Eternal Sleep

The Complete Edition

Hugo Jepsen

Chapters:

Eternal Sleep

The ocean waves keep beating
the rock solid parts of my heart
as if my self-destructive behaviour
was not enough to rip off my scars.

The blaze firing up at my shore,
and the calm before my own storm -
spars of wind confusing it all
but my life is what I'm fighting for.

These voices in my head,
they don't tell me how
to keep me above the safe -
What should I do right now?

At the precipice, I do stand,
but the weather puts me on my knees,
and I look up - stars in the sky -
tired but too young to go into an eternal sleep.

sinking in confusion

We've gathered here
to be crossing lines -
if destiny has the answer,
I'd give up my own life.

Somewhat, it's empathy
to run carefree with grace -
yet, you're so eager to make me stop,
it's like your hate for me ran out of place.

You've got a knack for ghosting
while giving me ghostly dreams -
as you write my name in your body,
I feel the dirt in my mouth as if you were burying me.

I didn't have the right answer for you,
so you sink me in deep confusion -
as if I didn't have it in myself to sink in it too.

shades of lipstick

Shades of lipstick in your tie,
ten colours of the lie I was told to -
I got mistaken for the smell of blood,
but you know, I'd never be with anyone but you.

You have looked for me in others
when I was dreaming of us together -
and everything would feel like a fairytale
but the pain of losing a life is that love isn't fair.

How have I tried to end all of what I feel?
Taking the blame, taking responsibility -
trying to be an honest man but the wild side
pulls me stronger than what I'd like it to be.

Shades of lipstick is blood spilt -
who did you kill if it wasn't me?

my sadness has become beautiful

When tears are running down,
I have found no ways to stop it -
it's from tears that I'm all about.

I held your hand, too strong, I think,
I find the pain to become quite beautiful,
but I don't think you share the same feeling.

And when my tears run over you,
you make it all about bad luck
instead of taking responsibility for the things you do.

Yet, I held your hand way too strong,
I think I didn't tell you that I was scared,
but I just wanted to keep me inside your chest.

let's move on for a happy ending

My world has changed,
my face doesn't look the same,
but when I look into your eyes,
I still feel the same way when I was alive.

But this love has finally passed away -
you got me but I got in the way.
He makes me feel like I should
but I would love you still if I could.

He does know all the reasons
for when I cry at night
and that's comforting nonetheless -
getting better at finding happiness.

Perhaps, I'm lying to myself
and all is happening as you said -
but it's time for you to move on
and hope that happiness never ends.

speechless words

I've covered myself
between the sheets -
the outdoors look better
if they never see me.

I see the light coming undone,
I've done nothing, yet always around -
when the raindrops take over my place,
it uncovers the secrets of my hometown.

I see the kindness in your evil,
I feel the depths of your soul
but you decided to stay
and I left the best person I've ever known.

Speechless words are also words -
I sit by the window, sitting in hurt,
tears seem to spill over my clothes -
I guess passion isn't the same as love.

約束 - promise

The days of laughing
and the days of hurt
found a way to just
heal by hugging each other.

And it has been a long time
since I let the sun touch my face.
I try to reach the light but I runaway -
if there's no shade, then, it's not safe.

Wanted to say a million things
but strength lacks at the back of my throat -
heartache has consumed all my emotions,
can't seem to feel that I'm heartbroken.

But the days of laugh
hug the days of pain -
and maybe, with love,
my hurt will go away.

lack of divine inspiration

Inspire beneath my desire
where my feet cannot go.
Inspire me beneath my breath
where words can be at my work.

And if for nothing, you've got the need
to put me to write for your purpose -
don't inspire me then - lack of divine inspiration.

killing me tonight

It hurts me so much within,
I just feel my heart getting thin,
And I feel a stroke inside of me,
I want to get out of me, away with it.

I feel some rainbows for real,
But I never accepted such a deal.
I feel some gold in your touch,
But it was never ever enough.

I feel some passion inside my bones,
But it was never really shown,
And I feel your warmth at night,
Even if you're sleeping outside.

And all the memories kept above
Are coming back so strong this time
That all I feel now is just love
And that love is killing me tonight.

I’ve been flying with a broken heart

Raise me up, give me a star,
I've been flying with a -
flying with a broken heart.

How do you think this is fair?
Believe, I'm alone, completely,
I need you to hear me out,
please, just don't judge me.

I've been crying but holding up,
I'll catch up the tears as they fall,
in my life, waiting is just a game,
the ocean cries but gives you salt.

Raise me up, take me afar from here,
home is not where I belong bleeding,
a safe haven is where you're near,
and if I'm not good enough, just leave,
just set me free, set me free, pretty please.

Lift me up, I've been flying with broken wings,
I held my thighs high up in the air with my arms,
I'm waiting for my death race to just start.

enticement as a dream

How long will I be this way?
How long? How long will I?
It's replicating emeralds inside -
will I feel the same way in July?

Shades of colour - black and blue -
if it's real or a dream, I'm not sure,
but when you take time to touch my soul,
my heart catches a feeling so peculiar.

If I take a swing on balancing it all out,
would you take my hand as support?
It would ache me if you decided to run away,
but also - what that love would be for?

How long will stay by my side?
Every step I take, my body takes a pause,
darkening the sights of my fear of time,
if all the enticement in me gets me lost.

Malibu home

At my Malibu home,
where I don't belong,
and even though, not alone -
I feel as if loneliness makes me strong.

Gaslight in the eyes, I can see,
because all that there is out there,
may be or may not be waiting for me.

Thunderstorms perched in the dark,
succulent desire to make it my own -
the future that doesn't belong to the past
is my way of telling myself that I've won.

But what if I haven't won, just yet?
What if all my way of apathy
is the way that I get upset?

luminescence

Luminescence in your body -
thinking about love when I run
freely in the wild with beasts next to me -
it's my luminescence wanting me to be free.

The walls of my room are overloaded
with your fingernail scratches and bites -
you try your best very best
to suck the hell out of my life.

I wonder how long, you've been in love
if you ever actually ever did -
you tame others' unique spirits
to meet your bloody needs.

The pain of losing me was
nothing compared to mine,
and that's all because,
you never looked into my eyes.

dance with death

There's too much blood
in the water of your bathtub -
you told me, you'd only take your life
if you could be real and drunk.

It's killing me when I wonder
about questions never answered,
promises that were never kept,
but here we are, once again.

Your kiss was all over my tie,
you make me, you make me
need to be dishonest and lie.
Why do you love me? Why?

The heart wants brutal rejection
to feel the pain of what is life -
you can always pick up the pace
and dance with death, side by side.

a thunder person

As if - as if your touch
meant something else -
it just touches my body,
but as if touch were words spelt.

My thunder crashing down on Earth -
right here, in a place where we stand,
my hand to yours, some innocence,
but stronger than that is your command.

And come to me, body and soul,
better than everything and all,
better than everything I've ever known.

One mirror to look at and two to merge,
but only one look can see right through
of everything that is going on between
me and you - just me and you.

the poem, right there (conclusion)

Some people want to know
but some don't –
We share the same soul
but some won't.

Bonus Chapters:

1. Boys Lie
2. Move On!
3. in a world that is not this one
4. visible cadence
5. Mercury Retrograde

Boys Lie

Boys lie, then they want revenge -
as if they were half of a man.
Then, they lie a little bit more,
as if I could ever understand.
Because truth to be told -
I do not honestly care.

Matured enough to withstand
words of false despair -
you tell me what I wanna hear
to, like magic, disappear.

Why have you told me
that love your religion?
The shades of a relationship
are something you couldn't envision.

Yet, you're still able to cry
when you keep up with your lies
to not look me in the eye.

Move On!

I am tired of being cautious
when all your lies feel nauseous.
Nothing was left for me to say -
hope to never see you one day.

When you cry, call it back luck -
hoping that we'd never break up.
When you think about calling me, you,
assume that I'm with somebody new.

What is your obsession?
It's time you learn your lesson.
You seem to turn on reckless
when somebody you once had
is in love with somebody else.

Your recent messages told me that
you're passing through a tough time
but I'm the one who doesn't have time to
tell you that moving on is what you should do.

in a world that is not this one

Once upon a time
as if I could ever go back
being happy as I once was.
Forgive me if I throw it away -
the past is all I've ever known.

If I pick up the footsteps
that I did leave behind -
If I forget what happened,
we would still be living in a lie.

That's not why I was born for -
cherished by mother and others,
to grow up, to catch dream by dream -
that's what you did mean
to me, but just to me.

Once upon a time, long ago,
in a world that is not this one -
you held my hand and I never let go.

visible cadence

Eyes glimpse metal
when everyone is around.
Thus, I do not command them -
body gestures and reflections alike -
don't kill me if one day, I'll die.

Ten heads come in -
fire blazes, forehead down -
what are they looking at, now?

From here to right there - distance -
near gazes make me feel them here.
Atrocious, no oxygen left to breathe -
are they the problem or is it me?

Up and beyond, time to leave it is -
trying to leave as nobody can see
where I am going to be -
but they, they did.

Mercury Retrograde

This ill luck is broken
as these words are spoken -
this ill fate will be changing
as this curse brokes like an omen.

A venture of silence for everything
that has happened in the past -
may those knives stick those
who have stabbed me in the back.

A little charm of love when these doors
of my own house become wide-open,
for all the love I've been running for
coming back as these words are spoken.

And I ask God, I ask the universe
to let me go on this Mercury retrograde
with easiness, with an untroubled ride
as I built my own little human fate.

Credits

Writer: Hugo Jepsen
Editor: Hugo Jepsen
Cover Creator: Hugo Jepsen
Image License: Unsplash
Publisher: Amazon

Disclaimer

Any resemblance to other creative projects is mere coincidence.

Copyrights

www.ingramcontent.com/pod-product-compliance
Lightning Source LLC
LaVergne TN
LVHW080600160826
845677LV00010B/1929

* 9 7 9 8 8 2 1 1 6 9 4 8 8 *